The Magnificent Garden

Written and Illustrated by

Kathy Cire

Dedicated to: Mary Caroline Cowden

On a quiet street, tucked far beyond the city, there lived a little girl and her family.

Every night the little girl would
crawl into her warm, cozy bed and
dream the most pleasant dreams.

And every morning when she awoke,
she would open her window and
breathe the sweet, fresh air.

As she glanced out her window and
was admiring the view, she noticed
something was missing.

That night she dreamed of the most
magnificent garden. A garden full
of flowers the colors of the rainbow.

The next day she realized what was missing as she looked out her window... A garden just like the one she had seen in her dreams.

So she began to clear a place to plant her garden. She worked all day planting seeds and nurturing her garden.

Several days later she woke up and looked out the window and saw the most magnificent garden she had ever seen.

There were flowers of all kinds.
Roses and daisies, lilies and
sunflowers...
Butterflies of all sizes and colors
came to sip the sweet nectar of the
flowers, and the little girl was happy.

One morning a large butterfly landed on her windowsill and whispered in her ear, "Hop on my wings and I will take you to the garden of joy!"

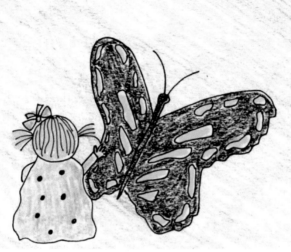

So the little girl hopped on the wings of the butterfly and they flew through the clouds to a place that felt just as warm and cozy as her little bed.

She loved this place so much that she asked the butterfly to give her wings.

So the little girl got her wings.

Soon she began to miss her family.
The butterfly said, "You can keep
your wings and go back to see your
family whenever you want."

So every day when the sun comes up
and shines on the little house tucked
far beyond the city, there is a
butterfly in the magnificent garden
that brings joy to everyone that sees
her.

And when her family catches a
glimpse of her... they are at peace.

Mary Caroline Cowden

We lost our beloved Mary Caroline, known to us as "MC," on October 12th, 2016 to a non-vaccine strain of bacterial meningitis. MC was SPECIAL and she lived all 362 days of her life with JOY and HAPPINESS, before she victoriously returned home to GOD.

We miss our MC desperately, but in our sorrow we do not ask, *"Why?"* instead we focus on, *"For what purpose?"* ... And that purpose is to reveal the GLORY of GOD. Instead of demanding an answer, we choose to TRUST in HIM, recognizing that our circumstances provide an opportunity to GLORIFY GOD by TRUSTING in his unseen purpose.

As we work to TRUST in the "unseen purpose," and look to continue MC's legacy of JOY and HAPPINESS, we dedicate the **12th DAY of EVERY MONTH** to be a day that we bring JOY to others ... just as MC brought JOY to our life!

So stop what you are doing - for just a minute - on the **12th DAY of EVERY MONTH** and do something to serve others. We challenge you to step outside of yourself and commit an act of kindness towards a stranger, volunteer during your lunch hour, call a friend who is struggling. All acts of kindness, big or small, will carry on MC's legacy of spreading JOY and HAPPINESS ... all while displaying the GLORY of GOD!

Go out and bring JOY to someone in honor of Mary Caroline Cowden on **12th DAY of EVERY MONTH and #MC12.**

May the GOD of HOPE fill you with all JOY and PEACE, as you TRUST in HIM, so that you may overflow with HOPE by the POWER of the HOLY SPIRIT. **Romans 15:13**

This book was written in honor of our
sweet Mary Caroline Cowden

Mary Caroline passed away suddenly on October 12, 2016 from the onset of a sudden illness. She laughed, smiled, and wore big bows, bringing joy and happiness to everyone. Mary Caroline ran the race that God had set for her 362 days and is continuing to complete it victoriously through organ donation. We know she is with God in heaven, and her spirit continues to give us strength.

My book was intended to give hope to families who have lost loved ones. The butterfly has become a symbol of comfort for our families. When we catch a glimpse of a butterfly, we are at peace.

Spread joy wherever you go!

53327105R00017

Made in the USA
Lexington, KY
30 September 2019